Original title:
The Meaning of Life, According to My Cat

Copyright © 2025 Creative Arts Management OÜ
All rights reserved.

Author: Julian Montgomery
ISBN HARDBACK: 978-1-80566-001-9
ISBN PAPERBACK: 978-1-80566-296-9

The Art of Napping

A sunbeam warms my furry frame,
In slumber, I seek my claim to fame.
The world drifts by, a distant sound,
In dreams, my kingdom knows no bounds.

A twist, a turn, a gentle sigh,
Paws tucked in, I watch clouds fly.
Moments pause, the clock stands still,
In cozy bliss, I've got my fill.

Furry Musings

Perched high up, I watch the scene,
Humans busy, so routine.
With a flip of my tail, I decree,
Life's simpler, come cuddle with me.

Why chase a dot when I can nap?
Socks and string? Now that's a trap!
In purrs and headbutts, I find my voice,
In this furry life, I rejoice!

The Mystery of the Midnight Pounce

Midnight strikes, I'm on the prowl,
Silently stalking, that's my growl.
A shadow moves—oh, what a thrill!
I pounce at shadows, it's my skill.

A leap from here, a twist in air,
The Wi-Fi box? It must beware!
Each night's a quest, a daring feat,
The world is mine, this cat can't be beat!

Scratching the Surface of Being

The scratching post stands tall and proud,
Every claw marks my feline crowd.
Is this my purpose? A point to make?
To leave my mark, for heaven's sake!

Each swipe a question, each pull a thought,
Of deep cat wisdom, sharply taught.
With fluff and purrs, I claim my space,
In this grand home, I own my place.

The Poetry of Purring

A warm spot on the sun,
That's where my day is won.
A nap is all I need,
In dreams, I make my creed.

Chasing shadows on the floor,
What lies beyond the door?
A world of endless play,
In my own feline way.

Cats and Cosmic Queries

Do the stars glare down at me?
Are they watching? Can't you see?
I ponder while I lick my paw,
What's really out there, just a flaw?

Do the mice hold all the keys?
In their tiny hearts, such peas.
Philosophy in every scratch,
I always find a way to hatch.

Whispers in the Meow

In every purr, a secret stirs,
With each meow, the cosmos purrs.
Life's a game of catch and chase,
I'm the master of this space.

From the window, I survey,
The entire world in disarray.
But here in my soft little chair,
I reign supreme, without a care.

Existential Fleas

What if life's just one big itch?
Scratching here, can be a glitch.
Fleas are tiny, yet they leap,
In this chaos, it's mine to keep.

Each nap a quest, profound yet brief,
In sunlit dreams, I find my relief.
I chase my tail, round and round,
In circles of thought, I am found.

Cozy Contemplation

On sunlit spots, I lay and dream,
With purring thoughts, as warm as cream.
A flick of tail, a gentle stretch,
A nap's embrace, my favorite sketch.

The humans rush with daily tasks,
While I find bliss in asking, "What masks?"
I ponder life through sleepy eyes,
With lofty thoughts and no goodbyes.

Lullabies of the Night

When night falls softly, I make my rounds,
A quiet hunter, no playful sounds.
With every creak that the house may yield,
I chase my dreams in the moonlit field.

Mice may fear their midnight plight,
But in my dreams, they bring delight.
Lullabies hum in shadows so deep,
While my fluffy form drifts off to sleep.

The Enigma of Catnip

A sprinkle here, a whiff right there,
Like magic dust, it fills the air.
I tumble, roll, and then I leap,
In fields of green, I lose my sleep.

Is life a game, a riddle to tease?
With kitty dreams that never freeze?
When high on joy, I roam my world,
A catnip leaf, my heart unfurled.

The Art of Being Aloof

To sit and stare, with regal ease,
With eyes that mean to put you at ease.
A flip of ears, a soft disdain,
For humans' love, not worth the strain.

Oh, look at me, so poised, refined,
While plotting mischief in my mind.
To rule this house, with gentle grace,
While feigning much, in this fine space.

Laughter in a Litter Box

A box of sand, my royal throne,
Each grain a jewel, each scoop, my own.
I dig and scratch, I leap and bounce,
In this tiny kingdom, I feel quite stout.

Why chase the mice? It's all a game,
The laughter lives where the dirt bears my name.
Pounce, roll, and dive, let the chaos begin,
In this realm of litter, I'm always the win!

Life Lessons from a Lap Cat

Curl up close, find comfort in warmth,
Look for the lap that feels like home.
Nap whenever, don't waste the chance,
In this cozy spot, life's a slow dance.

Demand some pets, with a paw and a purr,
Express your needs, make sure they confer.
Take life as it comes, with naps in between,
For in your warm lap, all is serene.

Paws and Thoughts

A window view, my throne of dreams,
Chasing shadows, or so it seems.
Life's a bird, I'll catch it one day,
Until then, I'll watch, while I play.

Thoughts of tossing, batting a string,
Joy in the simplest, petty little things.
With each little pounce, I learn and I grow,
The world is my stage, come watch the show!

Reflections on a Windowsill

Sitting high, where the sunbeams flow,
I watch the world, my very own show.
Birds flap by, oh how they tease,
An adventure awaits, if I only could leap!

A purr here, a stretch there, life's grand display,
I ponder on naps, and how to delay.
Life's simple pleasures, like warm rays at dawn,
On this windowsill throne, I flounce and yawn.

Moments Between Pounces

In sunbeams I lay, in blissful repose,
A kingdom of dreams, where the soft wind blows.
A twitch of my tail, then there's a quick dash,
The world becomes prey, oh, how I can thrash!

Each moment is mine, a delightful surprise,
I observe from my perch, with wise, watchful eyes.
My humans, they think they hold all the power,
Yet here on my throne, I reign every hour.

Claws, Curiosity, and Clarity

With claws that are sharp and a mind so keen,
I stalk the tall grass, like a cat on the scene.
Curiosity leads me on grand little quests,
From the depths of the couch to the tops of the nests.

A box can be treasure, a bag a great foe,
Every corner's a mystery, what's lurking? I'll know!
I leap and I dart, with such comic finesse,
While pondering life in my humble, soft dress.

Pondering the Purr

What is this sweet sound that rumbles within?
Is it magic? A trick? Or my cozy old kin?
When the world feels too loud, I curl up and hum,
In a blissful vibration, where all troubles come.

In each gentle purr lies a riddle or two,
A lesson in joy and in naps overdue.
My humans keep guessing, but they can't really see,
Life's sweetest moments reside here, just with me.

Furry Epiphanies

On the windowsill, I bask in the sun,
Like life's little riddle, I've only just begun.
Every twitch of my whiskers, every flick of my ear,
Carries whispers of wisdom, if only you'd hear.

I chase my own tail just to feel the sweet spin,
Each furry epiphany begins with a grin.
Life's not a distraction, it's filled with delight,
With snacks in my bowl, everything feels right!

The Stillness of a Catnap

In a sunbeam, I find my zone,
A slumber deep, a purring tone.
Dreams of fish and gourmet treats,
Life's most precious, cozy feats.

While you toil and stress all day,
I nap without a care or sway.
The world can wait, it's not my scene,
Just me and my dreams, so serene.

Navigating the Box of Life

Each box I find, a world unique,
A kingdom where I reign, so sleek.
It's not the size, but the delight,
In cardboard walls, I take my flight.

You see my box, but I see skies,
A treasure chest that multiplies.
With every leap, and every pounce,
In cardboard realms, I truly bounce.

Feline Intentions

I plot and plan, my tiny schemes,
To steal your lap, disrupt your dreams.
With a twitch of tail, I make my call,
You might be boss, but I'm the thrall.

A paw on you, a knowing glance,
My motives sly, a sneaky dance.
To claim your heart, my stealthy art,
In every nap, I play my part.

The Harmony of Hush

Quiet corners, where I rest,
Silence wraps me like a vest.
In the stillness, I feel alive,
In peace, my feline spirits thrive.

While chaos reigns outside my door,
I nap, I dream, and so much more.
For in my hush, the world's at bay,
I'm king of calm, and that's okay.

Whiskers of Wisdom

On sunlit perches, I survey,
The vast expanse where squirrels play.
A twitch of tail, a thoughtful pause,
In my domain, I am the cause.

The humans scramble for some peace,
While I just nap, my joys increase.
A purring hum, a cozy spot,
Decisions made? Why not, why not?

When dinner calls, I strut with flair,
A wise monarch in my plushy chair.
They serve my meals with such delight,
Life's simple pleasures, purest bite.

As shadows stretch and night descends,
I guard my realm, on me depends.
With moonlit dreams and playful beams,
A life of purrs and gentle schemes.

Paws and Philosophies

Cuddles and naps, my daily grind,
With soft, warm fur, I'm one of a kind.
The humans rush; I take my time,
In my slow world, I'm in my prime.

Curled in a ball, I ponder fate,
What's next on my plate? A splendid date!
My bowl's half-full, what can I say?
Life's an adventure in my own way.

The laser dot, a foe in sight,
A warrior's stance in playtime's light.
With swipes and leaps, I claim my fame,
Each little battle, a glorious game.

At end of day, in twilight's glow,
The world is mine; I put on a show.
Contentment reigns, I take a stance,
In nap time's grip, I find my chance.

Feline Insights at Dusk

A flick of my tail, the day recedes,
Pawing at shadows, fulfilling my needs.
In twilight's hush, I ponder deep,
The secrets of life, while humans sleep.

Each box I see, a realm to claim,
In every corner, I stake my name.
With whiskers twitching, I redefine,
My every conquest, a grand design.

The sound of crinkling, oh what a thrill,
As I inch closer, and wait, and still.
For the tiniest crumbles of joy do tell,
In simple pleasures, I find my spell.

With starlit skies above my head,
I slip away into dreams instead.
Purring softly, I ride the night,
In my cat kingdom, all feels so right.

Serene Sunbeams and Cat Dreams

Golden rays dance upon the floor,
I stretch and yawn, then I want more.
A sunbeam's warmth, a daily treat,
I strut in style on tiny feet.

Toy mice scattered, a warrior's quest,
In every pounce, I'm feeling blessed.
Life's a game, with fuzzy flair,
Who knew this life could be so rare?

The humans ask for daily chats,
I just meow, "What's up with that?"
For all they think they truly know,
I hold the wisdom, and steal the show.

At day's end, when the moon peeks through,
I curl in love, with skies of blue.
With slumber's grace, I chase my dreams,
In this feline world, nothing's as it seems.

The World from a Scratch Post

From high above, I survey the room,
With sunbeams warm, I conquer my doom.
A flick of my tail, oh what a view,
The world is my turf, just me and my crew.

My human thinks they run the show,
But I'm the star in this fabulous glow.
A napping king on my scratch post throne,
With dreams of fish, our meals are well known.

Chasing shadows like they're sly mice,
Bouncing like rubber; oh, isn't it nice?
Every corner holds a new surprise,
In my realm of purrs, wisdom lies.

What matters most? A sunbeam found,
With cozy naps and my favorite sound.
Life's just a game, full of delight,
With every pounce, I'm ready to fight.

Elegance in Simplicity

Bowls full of kibble, my daily delight,
Each morsel devoured, pure culinary height.
With a flick of my paw, I delight in the meal,
For a cat, it's a banquet, and I am the wheel.

A nap in a box, so snug and so warm,
Moments like these, they charge my charm.
Life's greatest joys wrapped in a ball,
Here's a tip, be a cat; you'll have a ball.

Chasing a speck does wonders for me,
I'm a playful ninja, wild and free.
With no care in the world, I prowl and sneak,
For a cat's simple pleasures, it's the peak of the peak.

When life's too fast and the humans do stress,
I curl up and purr; oh, what a mess!
In elegance found in the tiniest things,
You'll see joy's sweet tune as my heart sings.

Serenity in a Flick of a Tail

The world slows down with a flick of my tail,
Whiskers twitching; I'll never derail.
Calm in my kingdom, where silence reigns,
With a soft little purr, I shake off the chains.

Birds outside chirp, but I won't be swayed,
My spot on the windowsill never betrayed.
A lazy stretch, my zen garden grows,
As sunshine spills in, the tranquility flows.

Life ticks away in my fluffy cocoon,
Each afternoon nap feels like June.
Let the world rush by, I'm not in a race,
In every small moment, I find my grace.

A pounce on a leaf, their crinkling sound,
A moment of chaos in calmness profound.
With each little gesture and every grand leap,
I spread joy like magic, and slip into sleep.

Furry Graffiti on Life's Canvas

With every pawprint, a story unfurls,
In vibrant colors, I dance and twirl.
My fur on the couch, an abstract delight,
A masterpiece made in this cozy night.

Knocked over vases become my best shows,
Creating my art, where mischief just flows.
A flick of my tail, a canvas so bright,
I'm the furry Picasso; behold my slight!

Every scratch on the carpet tells tales of delight,
Of monsters I chased late into the night.
A trail of my fur is my signature flair,
For each wild adventure ignites a stare.

From dreaming in sunbeams to stealing your seat,
My life is a canvas, both messy and neat.
So celebrate all my furry graffiti,
For every little chaos is pure kitty-deity!

Serenity in a Pounce

A shadow darts across the floor,
A whiskered hunter, never a bore.
With each leap, joy is unfurled,
In my little kingdom, I'm the world.

Sunbeams warm my fluffy spot,
In this moment, worry forgot.
Chasing tails and dreaming wide,
In a cat's grace, I take pride.

A Dance of Paw Prints

Tiny steps on kitchen tiles,
A silent dance, a parade of smiles.
With each paw, a story spun,
In a world that's just for fun.

The moonlight glints on the floor,
I practice leaps, then beg for more.
A twist, a twirl, a playful bound,
Through shadows, my joy is found.

Whiskers of Wisdom

With every twitch of my feline face,
I hold the secrets of this place.
A nap, a stretch, purrs in the air,
Life's true lessons are found in the fair.

A wink to the sun as it starts to rise,
Chasing thoughts like birds in the skies.
Oh, the little things bring cheer,
From a gentle scratch to a heart so near.

Paws of Purpose

I knead the couch, every little spot,
In my realm, I'm the king—no doubt, no plot.
A playful flick of my feathery toy,
Happiness rolls in, a simple joy.

With each brisk chase of a shadowy gleam,
I remind you all to live the dream.
Life's a game, let's pounce and play,
In my furry world, it's always a good day.

Reflections in a Whisker

In a sunbeam lies my throne,
Fur and dreams are softly sown.
Treats are hidden, joys abound,
Life's a game; I'm king, I'm crowned.

From my perch, the world's a show,
Birds and bugs, my daily flow.
With a twitch of my tail, I decree,
Everything's perfect, just let it be.

Midnight Meditations

In the quiet of the night,
I plot my grand escape in flight.
The moonlit dance of shadowed mice,
Each chase is worth a thousand bites.

The humans sleep; I'm wide awake,
On soft paws, my stealth I make.
With a pounce and a playful leap,
Exploring more while they just sleep.

Nine Lives of Perspective

With nine lives to share my view,
Every corner's an adventure new.
I scale the heights of the tallest shelves,
Discovering treasures, like books and elves.

Each nap's a journey, each stretch's a quest,
From cozy warmth to a wild fest.
I see the world through curious eyes,
Every day brings a sweet surprise.

Catnip Chronicles

Oh, catnip fields, my heart's delight,
Rolling in bliss from day to night.
With a flip and a swish, I'm lost in glee,
Life's best moments are just for me.

I dash, I pounce, I prance around,
In my kingdom of fluff, I'm glory-bound.
Each sniff a tale, each leap a song,
In my cat world, I truly belong.

The Canvas of a Cat's Day

Upon the windowsill they lay,
Dreaming of fish and sunlit play.
Every shadow is a grand ballet,
With paws that tiptoe, come what may.

A sudden pounce on a paper ball,
Life's a game, they take it all.
With every leap, they have a ball,
In a world so big, yet so small.

Napping on warm, fuzzy chairs,
Chasing dust motes, with regal airs.
Every corner, a land of bears,
In a kingdom of laughs, they rule in pairs.

When dinner's served, it's quite the show,
They prance and prance, like there's a flow.
In this canvas, colors glow,
A life's delight in a feline flow.

In the Realm of a Furry Philosopher

Sitting sage on a high-worn throne,
Contemplating worlds unknown.
With a twitch of a tail, their wisdom shown,
In every nap, a truth is grown.

Eyes like jewels, they watch with grace,
The mysteries of this curious place.
With every blink, a measured pace,
Finding joy in a sunbeam's embrace.

Paws softly tread on soft-spun dreams,
Life's but a dance, so it seems.
From boxes to bags, an endless stream,
Philosophies wrapped in playful themes.

When they chase the dot of a laser light,
Existence is fun, pure delight.
In their paws, the cosmos feels right,
As starlit dreams unfold at night.

Seekers of Sunlit Spaces

Rays of gold in the afternoon,
Felines basking, a gentle tune.
In every beam, a sweet commune,
A world of warmth under the moon.

Cushioned in sun, they stretch and yawn,
Chasing shadows from dusk till dawn.
With a flick of their tail, their cares are gone,
In pursuit of warmth, they're never withdrawn.

Napping heroes on cozy beds,
Dreaming of fish and of warm-furred leads.
Each sunlit patch, where adventure spreads,
In a kingdom where laughter never treads.

With a playful leap, they claim their stake,
In a world so grand, make no mistake.
Every sunny corner, joys they awake,
In their realm, it's smiles they make.

A Trail of Whiskers

Whiskers twitch with curiosity,
Each corner holds a mystery.
In a playful dance, they roam so free,
Leaving laughter as their legacy.

On countertops where they don't belong,
With a sideways glance, they sing their song.
In every mischief, it feels so wrong,
But in their hearts, they can't go wrong.

With a flick, a twist, lives come alive,
In cardboard boxes, together they thrive.
In every pounce, their passions dive,
On a trail of whiskers, they always strive.

In the quiet of night, when all is still,
Dreams of chasing the moon give a thrill.
In every shadow, they find a will,
Leaving behind laughter, joy to fill.

Life Lessons on Four Legs

Chasing shadows, feeling bold,
Every corner's a story told.
Paws to the sky, I sit and stare,
Life's an adventure, I have no care.

Birds are gossipers, I must agree,
Their gossip travels fast and free.
A flick of my tail, a twitch of my ear,
I'm the spy in the house, never fear.

Sunbeams are secrets, too warm to keep,
I find my treasures in mid-day sleep.
With a purr that rumbles like thunder and rain,
I teach the humans joy without pain.

But watch your step, dear clumsy friend,
For my toys are traps that never end.
Life's a game, filled with surprise,
Just don't forget to scratch my thighs.

The Quest for the Perfect Nap

In the sunniest spot, I plot and scheme,
To find that elusive napping dream.
Soft blankets beckon, oh sweet embrace,
In my kingdom, I rule every space.

A shoe or a box, they're all fair game,
If it's cozy, I'll stake my claim.
The humans move, and I give them a stare,
Don't they know I'm the master of air?

Dreaming of tuna, a delight so grand,
In sleepy reveries, I take my stand.
Time stretches slowly, no need to rush,
Life's simple joys wrapped in a hush.

So hush now, please, let me drift away,
Tomorrow's adventures can start at midday.
With a twitch of a paw and a flick of my tail,
In the realm of dreams, I shall prevail.

Musings from a Cat Tower

From my perch high above the floor,
I watch the world; it's never a bore.
Humans bustle, they hurry and rush,
Yet here I sit, no need to hush.

Roaming my kingdom with regal grace,
Every nook and cranny is my own space.
I contemplate life from a vantage so high,
With just a leap, I'm the bird in the sky.

The dog down below, such a silly sight,
Chasing his tail in a comical fight.
I giggle softly, a purring delight,
In my world, I'm always just right.

When dinner's served, it's quite the affair,
A royal banquet, I simply must share.
Raise your glass, humans, don't be shy,
For in my heart, I'm the one who flies.

Whisker-Whispered Truths

The sun sets low, a golden hue,
Time for secrets, just me and you.
With every purr, a truth is told,
Life's a treasure, free and bold.

Sitting by windows, I watch the night,
Stars are my friends, shining bright.
They whisper stories of mice and grace,
Every flicker's a new embrace.

Humans dote, they try so hard,
To make me happy, but I'm in charge.
With a flick of my paw and a turn of my head,
I shape their world, while they're still in bed.

So heed my words, dear friend divine,
Life's not a hassle; it's a winding line.
In every nap and playful attack,
The secrets of happiness, I'll never lack.

Shadows of the Litter Box

In a world of littered dreams,
My cat plots with sly little schemes.
Each paw a shadow, swift and spry,
As he emerges, oh so sly.

With a flick of his tail, he reigns,
Claiming territories, oh what gains!
The box his kingdom, of utmost pride,
Where dignity and fur collide.

He ponders life with each soft scratch,
In friendly dust, he finds his match.
A throne of sand where worries fade,
In his wise gaze, all doubts are laid.

What's beyond the walls? He does not care,
For here in the box, he rules the air.
A world of wonder, with paw prints spread,
In his cozy realm, life is well led.

Reflections on a Cat's Leap

He sits and stares at heights above,
A leap of faith, a cat's true love.
With grace he bounds, a furry dart,
Landing softly, pure feline art.

The couch, the curtain, all in sight,
Each jump's a quest, a thrilling flight.
He knows the world is his to claim,
With each brave leap, he plays the game.

Physics? Oh please, they have no hold,
For cats defy what we're told.
With a wiggle and a flick, he's airborne,
In his merry dance, he's reborn.

Yet when he lands, it's all a show,
Pretending he meant it; oh, what a pro!
Each leap a riddle, full of grace,
In this grand circus, he takes his place.

The Zen of Tail-Chasing

Round and round the tiny paws go,
The tail is the star of this absurd show.
With big, wide eyes and a twitchy nose,
In dizzy circles, he spins, he doze.

What wisdom lies in this furry race?
Too deep for words in a playful chase.
With leaps and bounds, the world spins fast,
Yet in his play, he finds contrast.

The chasing ceases with a gentle flop,
In a tangle of fur, he'll finally stop.
With a yawn and a stretch, life slows down,
In the simple chase, he wears no crown.

It's the joy of the moment, the whirling delight,
In the chase of his tail, nothing feels right.
Yet from chaos comes peace, as he closes his eyes,
Finding wisdom where silliness lies.

Paws and Possibilities

With paws to tread where dreams unfold,
Every corner's a story waiting to be told.
A sunbeam's warmth, a paper's crinkle,
Adventures begin with every blink and wrinkle.

On the windowsill, he dreams of flight,
Wishing to stretch to infinite height.
Chasing shadows with a gentle strut,
In a world so grand, he will not be shut.

A box to explore, or a plant to nibble,
With curious eyes, he will not quibble.
Each day's a gift packed with surprise,
Life's clever paths, he'll always devise.

In his kingdom of leisure, he finds his bliss,
Every cuddle, each cheeky kiss.
For in his heart, he knows one thing,
Every moment counts, let the joy ring!

The Art of Napping

In sunbeams I sprawl, it's my favorite spot,
A world of dreams, where I'm never caught.
With paws tucked in tight, I drift into bliss,
What more could I want? I wouldn't miss this!

The vacuum roars loud, but I hardly care,
Let it scream, let it shout, I'll still be right there.
In deep slumber's embrace, I reign supreme,
Life's little troubles are just a bad dream.

A twitch of my tail, a purr here and there,
I'm the king of my castle, the throne is my chair.
When dinner time comes, I'll wake with delight,
But first, one more nap—it's my favorite rite!

So heed my wise words, take time to unwind,
In the cozy embrace of the nap that you find.
For life is a catnap, sweet peace we will share,
Dreams are the secrets that linger in air.

Shadows and Silhouettes

A shadow at play, in the afternoon light,
I chase my own form, what a silly sight.
On the wall, I leap with such grace and flair,
A master of forms, in the sun, I declare!

The pounce, oh so bold, on that unsuspecting fly,
A delicate dance; I'm the ruler, oh my!
With every small leap, I redefine cool,
In my kingdom of shadows, I reign like a fool.

The curtains, they flutter, I stalk with great pride,
A ninja in stripes, with nowhere to hide.
I'll ambush my realm, from the chair to the bed,
As the world is my playground, I'll conquer it, said!

And when night descends, with its moonlit glow,
My silhouette triumphs in the soft evening flow.
In the dance of the dark, my antics unfold,
Life's just a game, always funny, never old.

Curled Up in Contemplation

Curled up so tight in my plush little nest,
I ponder my days, and which nap is best.
A taste of sweet tuna? Or sun-warmed delight?
The mysteries of life fill my mind every night.

Oh, to be a potted plant, to sip sunlight slow,
Or maybe a feathery mouse on the go!
With dreams of my conquests drifting in air,
I find pure contentment in this soft, cozy lair.

What should I conquer next? The couch or the rug?
Or perhaps I'll embark on the hunt for a bug?
For life's but a puzzle, a glorious quest,
To nap, eat, and play—oh, I'm truly blessed!

So roll with the giggles and bask in the sun,
For the world through my eyes is a whimsical fun.
With each little thought, I stretch, yawn, and beam,
Life is a fantasy, perfect as a dream.

Beyond the Catnip Rainbow

Atop my cat tree, I survey my great land,
With catnip in sight, I plot and I plan.
A sprinkle of magic, a leap to the sky,
In my feline kingdom, oh how time does fly!

I roll in the grass, in the scent of delight,
With paws full of mischief, I dance in the night.
A flick of my tail, and I soar through the air,
A superhero cat—everyone stop and stare!

When moonlight does whisper, and stars seem to twinkle,

I dash through the halls, oh, I'm quick as a sprinkles!
Each corner a mystery, each shadow a game,
In the land of catnip, nothing feels the same.

So dream on, dear humans, in your world so bright,
While I chase the rainbows with pure feline might.
For life is a journey, a crazy, wild run,
And I'm the main character, just look how I've spun!

Serenade of Soft Steps

In twilight's glow, I creep so sly,
With whiskers twitching, I prance and fly.
A cornered shadow, a beacon of thrill,
My mission: pouncing, with claws at will.

The world is vast, my kingdom wide,
Each rustle beckons, my playful guide.
A flick of the tail and I'm off like a dart,
In every small chaos, I find my part.

In the Company of Felines

In a sunbeam's warmth, I claim my throne,
Surveying my subjects, I feel quite grown.
Napping together, we form a pile,
Dreaming of tuna and a sunny smile.

With a swat of my paw, I declare it's time,
For a dance of delight and a silly rhyme.
The humans all laugh, they think it's odd,
But in our own way, we purr and applaud.

Scratches of Serenity

Oh, the softest spots beneath my chin,
A gentle scratch welcomes my purring din.
Life's greatest treasures, I have them all,
A cozy lap is my cushy hall.

The couch is my canvas, I'll knead and I'll tread,
Leaving my mark where the humans have spread.
With a flick of my tail, I reign supreme,
In this world of comfort, I live my dream.

The Joy of Feathered Toys

A feathered delight, it dangles and sways,
I leap and I twirl, in marvelous plays.
With a pounce and a bound, I am swift, I am sly,
Chasing my dreams as they flutter and fly.

Oh, what a game of hunt and of chase,
Each playful moment, I'm quick to embrace.
With my eyes all a-glow and my spirit so spry,
These simple joys lift my heart to the sky.

Wisdom in Every Stray

In sunlit spots I take my naps,
A wise old feline with plenty of laps.
Chasing shadows, I ponder the day,
What do humans do, while I nap away?

With every purr, I share my thoughts,
I rule the house, or at least I ought.
The humans worship my every meow,
They don't know my secret: I run the show now!

A flick of my tail, they scatter like mice,
I lounge in luxury; isn't that nice?
Life's a game of stealth and delight,
Why rush through the day when I can sleep tight?

So here I sit, the king of the kloof,
Observing my realm from the top of the roof.
In the grand scheme of things, who needs a plan?
Just keep the treats coming; I'm a happy cat, man!

Through Littered Paths

In a world of boxes, I am the sage,
Every corner reveals a new stage.
A paradise built on crinkly sounds,
With litter and toys scattered all around.

I leap and I pounce on invisible foes,
While humans just smile, who knows what I knows?
Every dust mote is a dragon to spar,
I'll conquer them all, I'm a feline star!

Life is a hunt, full of exciting quests,
The world is my kingdom, I'm always the best.
A swift little dash, and I'm off in a flash,
Reality fades—oh! what's that, a sash?

So I prance through the chaos, with paws free of care,
Each moment a treasure, a whimsical flare.
Who needs a map when your senses are keen?
In a littered world, I'm the cat of the scene!

Fluffy Contemplations

As I gaze out the window, deep in thought,
I'm pondering things that matter a lot.
Is there more to life than a warm sunny spot?
Or the crinkle of bags that my humans forgot?

With each little purr, comes wisdom so grand,
Scratch me behind ears; you'll understand.
Chasing my tail is a philosophical chase,
Perhaps life's a circle, a continuous race?

I watch as they scurry, my humans in haste,
Their busy little lives involve little taste.
My treasures are fluffy, and I enjoy,
A moment so simple gives me pure joy!

So let's fill our days with silliness bright,
Pounce on the curtains and leap into night.
Each day is a canvas, so vivid, so bold,
In my fluffy world, the wonders unfold!

The Countdown to Dinner

The clock strikes six, it's my favorite chime,
It's nearly my dinner, the moment sublime.
I stalk the kitchen, graceful and spry,
With hopeful paws and a glint in my eye.

Those humans may think that they rule the roost,
But at dinner time, oh, I am the truth.
A flick of my whiskers, a soft little meow,
They shuffle my way, oh yes, watch them bow!

As bowls hit the floor, I dash like a pro,
Gourmet delights, it's my grand culinary show.
With each precious bite, I savor the fate,
Life's greatest pleasure comes served on a plate.

So here's my advice, dear friends, come and see,
The secret of happiness? It's finding the key—
A tasty dish, some snuggles, and a nap!
Reflecting on life while curled in a lap.

The Nonsense of a Cat's Play

A feather dangles, sways and spins,
With pounces poised, the fun begins.
A shadow caught, a leap so bold,
In this grand show, my heart's consoled.

The world is wide, yet small my space,
I chase my tail—a silly race.
The box that came? A throne, it seems,
In cardboard realms, I plot my schemes.

A crumpled ball, my prized delight,
With every toss, it takes to flight.
Oh, what a joy in simplest play,
This is my job; I earn my pay.

As day turns night, my kingdom sprawls,
The silent halls, my evening calls.
With each wild chase, each bounding leap,
In nonsensical joy, I softly sleep.

A Symphony of Purrs and Paws

In moonlit hours, a soft refrain,
A gentle purr, like falling rain.
Each whiskered note, a sweet surprise,
Resounding softly, where my heart lies.

With paws that dance on quiet floors,
I conduct symphonies—open doors.
The world outside? A distant hum,
But here I reign, I am the drum.

The scratching post, my finest stage,
A furry diva, I engage.
With every leap, my spirit sings,
In feline sounds, the joy it brings.

So let the night be filled with cheer,
The music of paws is all I hear.
In symphonies of curls and bliss,
This cat's life, I will not miss.

Furry Tales of Introspection

Upon the windowsill, I gaze,
At passing birds and sunny rays.
With thoughtful poise and a twitching tail,
I ponder life—a curious tale.

Is there a quest beyond this nap?
A world of dreams beneath my cap?
Each sunny spot a kingdom made,
In furry tales, I play my trade.

I watch the humans, so they race,
Through busy days, a frantic chase.
Yet here I lounge, without a care,
In deep reflections of my lair.

With every stretch and blissful sigh,
I find my truth—not asking why.
For in each scratch and gentle touch,
I've learned that life is simply… such.

Catnip Dreams and Nighttime Thoughts

Under the stars, my mind takes flight,
With catnip dreams that fill the night.
A swirling vortex, a fragrant tease,
In this soft haze, I drift with ease.

I chase the wisps of scents unknown,
In fields of green, I'm not alone.
The moon a friend, the sky a song,
In these sweet thoughts, I can't go wrong.

Shadows dance upon the floor,
Adventures wait behind each door.
With the soft grace of twilight's hush,
I plot my course—no need to rush.

So here's to dreams, both wild and true,
In nighttime musings, I find my clue.
With paws tucked close, and heart at peace,
In catnip realms, may joy increase.

Tails of Existence

In the sun, I stretch and yawn,
Chasing shadows as the dawn.
A flick of tail, a playful pounce,
On fleeting dust, I take my chance.

Napping here is pure delight,
Dreaming of the next big bite.
Oh, the world is mine to claim,
As my humans call my name!

A cardboard box is paradise,
Within its walls, I roll and slice.
Jumps and leaps, a gymnast's feat,
For me, the world is oh so sweet!

Life's a game, with yarn to chase,
In my realm, there's no disgrace.
The antics of a furry king,
Indulge in every little thing.

In Search of Sunbeams

I roam the house, in quiet quest,
For warm sun patches, that's the best.
With a squint, I savor the rays,
As my feline wisdom stays.

My humans fret, they don't quite see,
That simple joy is all I need.
A head tilt here, a gentle purr,
Life's a breeze when I confer.

The window sill is my throne fair,
I watch the world without a care.
Birds outside, a fleeting dance,
Oh how they wish to share my chance!

From birdwatching to long cat naps,
Every moment, a gentle flap.
In sunbeams' glow, my heart's set free,
In this warm world, it's just me.

A Cat's Perspective

I wonder why you rush and race,
When all I need is my cozy space.
The world spins fast, yet I will wait,
A nap can lead to something great.

A rustle here, a crinkle there,
Life's small wonders, I do declare.
Each cardboard box, a brand new land,
In my own realm, I take a stand.

The laser dot, my greatest foe,
A cunning creature, swift and slow.
I leap and dart, a feline ghost,
Yet it evades me, I am lost!

My masters laugh, they feed me treats,
While plotting schemes and sneaky feats.
In this grand play, I lead the way,
A king in fur, day after day.

Silent Reflections of Fur

In dusk's embrace, I sit and stare,
A little fluff with time to spare.
Thoughts like shadows glide and flow,
In silent musings, I softly glow.

What lies beyond the realm I roam?
This chair, this lap, it feels like home.
With every scratch, I knead my dreams,
In cozy naps, life's grand schemes.

The humans chatter, I simply blink,
With every gaze, I share a wink.
Their secrets told in warm caress,
But I, the sage, know they're a mess!

As night descends, I stroll the halls,
An echo of my soft-footed calls.
In purrs, I weave my legacy,
A whisper of fur, a mystery.

A Feline's Philosophy

Sunbeam spots are prime real estate,
Chasing dust motes is truly fate.
Nap, pounce, and then repeat,
Life's a game, so feel the heat.

Peeking out from cardboard caves,
Every box, a treasure saves.
Dinnertime is always grand,
One paw raised, a tiny hand.

Friendly shadows come alive,
Watch the humans strive and strive.
Step on keys, they jump and yell,
My kingdom's rule, oh so well.

The world is mine, and I reign free,
Sipping tuna-flavored tea.
Witty glances, tail held high,
Life's absurd, and so am I!

Nine Lives, One Truth

Nine lives in a single day,
Chasing tails and toys that play.
Slippers are the ultimate foe,
Pouncing hard, it's always a show.

Snoozing on your favorite chair,
With a noble, regal air.
A twitch of whiskers, oh so sly,
One quick leap, I own the sky.

Stray from routine? Never, how?
Belly rubs? Just do it now!
A can of fish is throne-worthy,
Snack attack, oh so swervy!

Climbing curtains, why not dare?
Surveying from the highest stair.
With lazy grace, I rule the night,
In my world, everything's right!

Through My Cat's Eyes

Outside the window, birds all chat,
Life's a show, and I'm so fat!
Flicking tails, with laser focus,
Pounce and nap, it's all hocus pocus.

Boxes stacked? A climb I'll scale,
With every jump, I will prevail.
Human laughter? Makes me pout,
What's the fuss? I'll figure it out.

Chasing after that dot of light,
Turns a lazy day to sheer delight.
Curling up on a sock pile,
I wear your scent like my best style.

Through my eyes, the world's a jest,
Charming chaos is the best.
With every stretch and every yawn,
I declare it's time to fawn!

Purring Profound

In a world of endless grace,
Felines roam at their own pace.
Silken fur, a soothing balm,
Every purr a perfect calm.

The neighbor's dog, what a bore!
Feeling regal, I simply snore.
On the counter, stealing treats,
Clever plans, none can defeat.

Youthful leaps, and then a sigh,
Life's profound—just watch me fly!
Cuddles from you, I do adore,
Keep petting me; I'll beg for more.

With every blink, I just reveal,
Those secret truths that make me feel.
In cozy naps and playful spins,
This joyous life, oh, where it begins!

Purring through Existence

A soft purr in the morning light,
I lay on your lap, everything feels right.
Chasing dust motes, a thrilling race,
Sunbeams warm my furry face.

Life's a nap, then it's playtime,
Dodge the vacuum, isn't it sublime?
Scratch a post, claim my throne,
In this kingdom, I'm not alone.

Dinner's served—oh, what a feast!
Two-legged chef, you're the best, at least!
With a flick of the tail and a wink,
Life's a story—paws are the ink!

So let's cuddle and watch the show,
From the couch, I really steal the glow.
With treats and toys, I live so grand,
This little world is perfectly planned.

A Window to the World

From my perch, I see it all,
Squirrels scamper, and birds do call.
A world so big, so fast, so wide,
Yet here I sit, my feline pride.

I chase shadows and dart at flies,
With curious eyes and silly sighs.
Each glance outside, a grand delight,
I'm the queen of my lofty height!

What's that noise? Oh, it's just the mail,
I'll defend us both, I'll never fail!
With a mighty howl and a fierce glare,
The postman's skills? I simply don't care!

As the sun sets, I yawn and dream,
Of chasing ducks along a stream.
In my window seat, life is sweet,
A watchful eye on the world's heartbeat.

Tails of Truth on Quiet Nights

When day turns to dusk, the room gets still,
I curl on your lap, it gives me a thrill.
With a flick of my tail and a sleepy glance,
I ponder my life—what a wild dance!

With each little scratch behind the ear,
Comes knowledge profound and crystal clear.
Why chase the laser, why chase the red?
Life is about these snuggles instead!

Unlimited snacks, and cozy beds,
Endless naps fill our gentle threads.
These quiet nights, the moon's soft glow,
Are the moments I cherish, oh don't you know?

In dreams, I leap and pounce on stars,
From the couch to the fridge, I'll venture far.
With paws on your heart, let's drift away,
In our world, each night becomes play.

Musings from the Litter Box

In the corner, where secrets hide,
I sit and ponder with feline pride.
Life's messy, but that's quite okay,
I strike a pose and confidently sway.

With little clumps, I compose my art,
From straw and shavings, I'll play my part.
This throne of mine, a kingdom fine,
Where thoughts are deep and peace aligns.

Each scoop reveals what lies beneath,
Digging up gems, my own little wreath.
Philosophy's grand in my tiny domain,
And each little pawprint's my own refrain.

So here I sit, with a wise, sly glance,
Life's a litter box - it's a playful dance.
Dig deep, my friend, and you just might see,
Truth in the chaos, my philosophy!

A Universe in a Cat's Gaze

In a sunbeam, I take my throne,
Worlds unfold in each soft purr.
Plenty of naps, that's how I own,
Chasing shadows, I'm the blur.

A flick of my tail, the world's delight,
Birds in the sky, how I wish to fly.
With each graceful leap, I touch the night,
The cosmos dances, oh my, oh my!

A yarn ball rolls, chaos ensues,
It's a grand adventure, without a doubt.
Loyal subjects scatter like morning dew,
In my kingdom, I'm the cat, no doubt.

Gazing deep into empty space,
I ponder questions none can know.
Will they serve me treats or hide my face?
Ah, the true beauty of this show.

Dances in the Moonlight

Underneath the silver glow,
I prance upon the kitchen floor.
With a stealthy leap, I perform my show,
A dance that leaves you wanting more.

My paws whisper secrets to the night,
Chasing the beams with all my might.
Each twirl and wiggle feels just right,
A ballet for you, a pure delight.

The broomstick's my partner, oh so grand,
Together we sweep, we fly, we spin.
Every corner's a stage, you understand,
In this feline tale, I always win.

As you watch, chuckling at my moves,
Just remember, I lead the game.
Life's a dance, and I find my grooves,
In moonlit magic, I stake my claim.

Beyond the Bowl

They say that food is all I seek,
But there's more to my fanciful mind.
A long cat nap and a game of sneak,
In every corner, there's treasure to find.

A box left open? It's my new launch,
Exploring realms both near and far.
Each crinkle, each scratch, a royal haunch,
In my kingdom, I'm the shining star.

Oh, but look! A dust mote floats by,
How enchanting, dancing in air.
With a paw, I pounce, I leap, I fly,
In the simple joys, I'm always aware.

So while I nibble my dinner with glee,
Remember, adventures await beyond, see!
Life's a buffet, there's more to decree,
With endless fun, I freely respond.

The Heartbeat of the House

In cozy corners, I reign supreme,
Purring softly, I set the tone.
Every person needs a feline dream,
To keep their hearts from turning to stone.

I sit on laps, a warm, soft ball,
Rolling in treasures, oh what a show!
With gentle nudges, I inspire all,
To pause and cherish, to love and grow.

Every scratch behind my ears ignites,
A bond that's strong, forever true.
With my whiskers twitching in the nights,
I'm the laughter, the joy, the glue.

For when you're weary from life's race,
Look down, I'm there, a confidant.
With a flick of my tail, I'll fill the space,
In my fluffy world, all is nonchalant.

Cuddles and Cosmic Conundrums

In sunbeams, I stretch wide,
Pondering the great quest,
Chasing shadows and light,
Where naps might be the best.

Jumps and tumbles in the air,
With grace, I land with flair,
Life's a game of catch me, please,
Does it matter? I'm just here to tease.

My humans think they rule the day,
But I am the king, that's my way,
With every curl, I take my throne,
In this universe, I'm not alone.

So keep your questions and your doubts,
Just feed me well, and I'll lounge about,
Life's a ball of yarn and more,
Just let me snooze; I adore!

Hidden Treasures Beneath the Couch

Beneath the couch, oh what a find,
A fortress of fluff, treasures combined,
Crumbs from snacks and lost old toys,
   A kingdom fit for clever boys.

I dive right in, paws digging deep,
Here lies the secrets that I keep,
Each lost tidbit—a gourmet meal,
   Every find just adds to my zeal.

Humans say they seek the truth,
But all I need is hidden loot,
A chew toy here, a tiny bell there,
   In this realm, I've not a care.

So while you ponder worldly things,
I'll chase my tail and sprout my wings,
Let life be fun, with no regrets,
   In my cozy cave, I have no debts!

Curiosities of Catkind

What's that rustle? What's that sound?
A leaf? A bug? Adventure abound!
I'm off to investigate every nook,
With stealthy grace, just like a crook.

Why do humans stare at screens?
When out the window are birds, and greens?
I'll bat at shadows, and spy with glee,
Curiosity lives inside of me.

A box appears; it must be mine,
I'll curl right up, it's perfectly fine,
Life's a maze, a playful jest,
In cuddly corners, I find my rest.

Each day brings wonders, small and bright,
For us cats, it's pure delight,
So with every pounce, I live and laugh,
At life's silly, strange autograph.

Wisdom from the Whiskers

Wisdom flows from whiskers long,
In each flick, there lies a song,
Patience rules as birds go by,
I watch, I plot, oh me, oh my!

A sunny spot is not just fate,
It's where I think, it's where I wait,
My tiny kingdom, soft and warm,
In this embrace, I find my charm.

So let them work and toil away,
While I master the art of play,
With every nap, I gain my might,
In the hustle, I'm out of sight.

Remember this, oh human friend,
Life's joys are found where moments blend,
Embrace the naps, the twists, the spins,
In every whisker, laughter wins!

Laughter in a Meow

In the sun, I stretch and nap,
My life is simple, no need for a map.
With a flick of my tail, I reign supreme,
Chasing dust motes, living the dream.

Sometimes I plot on the window's edge,
Staring at birds, I make my pledge.
To nap for hours, then spring into action,
My fuzzy antics cause great distraction.

Each pounce and leap, a dance of delight,
I'm an acrobat in the soft, warm light.
With every meow, I spark a cheer,
Who needs a job when I've got this career?

Oh, the silly humans I call my crew,
They laugh at my antics, what else can they do?
In my world of whiskers, laughter's a must,
In frolicking fur, I surely trust.

Quest for the Perfect Sunbeam

The morning sun comes flooding in,
I'll chase that light, it's where I begin.
From sofa to sill, I roam with grace,
In search of warmth, my favorite place.

Dancing shadows can't steal my glow,
I'll lie here, thank you, just so you know.
With a belly-up pose, I bask in delight,
My quest for warmth, a glorious fight.

Each sunbeam just seems to call my name,
All around the house, a sunbeam game.
When I find the spot, I'll claim with a purr,
For I am the champion, the ultimate blur.

So let the world spin and humans fret,
I'll nap in my beam, no need to sweat.
In my kingdom of sunlight, I rule with my charm,
Seeking warmth, I find my calm.

A Symphony of Purrs

In the warm lap, I start to vibrate,
With a purr so soft, it's never too late.
Melodies flow, a husky refrain,
In every tickle, I let joy reign.

Mysterious tunes echo from my chest,
A symphony grand, I am truly blessed.
With a gentle nudge, I play the key,
Harmony found between me and thee.

Watch my whiskers dance when you scratch my chin,
A concerto of whispers when the fun begins.
Join me in music, let laughter arise,
In this playful chorus, joy fills the skies.

From rolling on floors to leapfrogging chairs,
Each note is a step on the path that we share.
Life's silly tunes echo loud and clear,
In the symphony of meows, love's always near.

The Secrets of the Stairs

Oh, the stairs, they hold so much intrigue,
A mystery where my daring takes league.
One careful step, then I sprint with glee,
I leave all my worries, feel wild and free.

Up I go, with a leap and a bound,
Each step whispers secrets I haven't found.
The world below seems tiny and far,
A feline explorer, my own shining star.

At the top, I survey my domain,
Like a mighty ruler, no hint of disdain.
I plot my descent, with dignified grace,
Then pounce on a human, oh what a chase!

Back down I scamper, with a flick of my tail,
Stairs are adventure; they never grow stale.
So here's to the heights where the fun never ends,
Life's full of surprises, especially with friends.

The Hunt for Happiness

In shadows I creep, a silent parade,
Chasing dust motes, my grand escapade.
A flick of the tail, a leap to the wall,
Happiness waits where the toys seem to sprawl.

The world is a playground, filled with delight,
A cardboard box moonlit on a starry night.
With each thrilling pounce, and each wild chase,
Joy is unfurled in the silliest place.

Feathers and strings hold my fleeting glee,
In the simple embrace of a warm sunny spree.
Life is a journey when the treats are divine,
With every small nibble, the universe shines.

So I'll stalk and I'll prance, in my fluffy disguise,
For happiness winks from the scurrying flies.
In every grand hunt, in each whimsical chance,
I find life's true rhythm in frolic and dance.

Fleeting Moments of Grace

A sunbeam arrives, and I stretch out wide,
With each lazy yawn, I beckon the tide.
In that golden glow, time seems to pause,
I bask in the warmth, without any cause.

A fluttering leaf, a rustling sound,
In my kingdom of pillows, serenity found.
I leap and I twirl, with elegance rare,
Life's little marvels float through the air.

With twitching whiskers, I ponder the play,
Of fleeting moments that whisk me away.
In a blink, I see joy in the softest purr,
As life dances by in a whiskered blur.

So here I reign, with a paw on my throne,
In the theater of grace, I'm never alone.
With mischief and mirth, and love's gentle trace,
Each day's a fine stage for my delicate grace.

Claws and Clarity

Each tiny scratching post, a shrine of wisdom,
My claws etch the truths of feline freedom.
With every small mark, I lay down my dreams,
Life's more than it seems, or so it seems.

The world spins around while I sharpen my skills,
In the quest for clarity, I seek playful thrills.
A swat at a shadow, a chase in the night,
I find my own balance in the dance of delight.

In sun-drenched corners, I ponder my fate,
Where a nap becomes deep as my thoughts animate.
I unravel the secrets of time with a yawn,
Content with my musings till the break of dawn.

So here I am, wise beyond my soft fur,
With claws ready to scratch at the things that occur.
In my playful pursuit, clarity comes near,
Through a lens of mischief, each moment is clear.

Furry Philosophers Speak

Gather 'round friends, for we're wise but aloof,
Furry philosophers on a rooftop.
With twinkling eyes and paws on our chins,
We ponder the secrets, where laughter begins.

Is life but a bowl filled with crunchy delight?
Or the thrill of the hunt on a soft, cozy night?
We debate the great questions, tails swishing with flair,
In a world of our making, we sing without care.

Though the humans may laugh, and roll their eyes wide,
It's we who hold wisdom, with dignity and pride.
A twitch of a whisker, a well-timed meow,
Our profound musings tie up the here and the now.

So heed our soft wisdom, from the floor to the chair,
Life's greatest pursuit? A sunbeam to share.
With cuddles and purring, our truths we'll impart,
In a language so clear, it's the rhythm of heart.